TRUANT

Edited by Nate Lippens

Pilot Press
London

"I think there's something about falling out of the world, falling out of the conventional world, being literally in the margins that does feel to me like it's a kind of queer sensibility."

- Olivia Laing in conversation with Matt Wolf, BOMB

'Maybe someday we will find refuge in true reality. In the meantime, can I just say how opposed I am to all of this?'

- Alejandra Pizarnik, The Possessed Among the Lilacs

Character Studies

The Traveler

Years ago. An overnight ferry (Athens to Crete) docked just as the sun was coming up, and I clambered off like everyone else, my one large bag strapped awkwardly to my back, resting on the concrete to get my bearings, back on land. A young man not far from me tossed his bag gently on the ground, sat on it, opened a pack of cigarettes, lit one, and seeing me see him, offered me one with a raised eyebrow, thrusting the pack in my direction. I waved my hands in a no-thanks gesture, but feeling some pressure to return the kindness, I said to him, "Nice morning."

"Yes it is," he said, in clear English with what I think was a Spanish accent. "Where are you headed?"

"I don't really know," I said, suddenly realizing I was nervous about having nowhere to stay, suddenly concerned that my nervousness might be showing. "I don't even know where I'm staying yet. I haven't booked a room—haven't booked anything."

He looked at my face. He took a long drag and then held the cigarette out in front of his chest, as if to examine it, and he said to me, "Ah, but that's the best part."

He stood up, slung his bag across his shoulder, and walked off, flashing me a quick peace sign.

I watched his figure get blurrier and smaller with distance. The sun was not yet up, but darkness was losing its grip on the day. Who was this traveler, this person at peace with the absurdity and the aleatoric nature of the world. Who was this person, practically winking at me, telling me to loosen up, to go wherever the universe took me?
For the entire trip, I hoped to see him somewhere, sitting at some cafe reading a book, browsing the vegetable stands for a fresh tomato, drinking a beer at some bar.

I never saw him again.

The Queen

"But you must understand," she said to the young woman beside her, "if you are too beautiful they'll want to kill you. I don't mean murder you, though that might happen. I mean they will want to make you normal, and you'll have to decide whether or not they're right. Real beauty is always outlawed."

The girl blinked quickly, as though she were struggling to take in everything the old woman had said.

The old woman began rifling through her small handbag. She kept her handbag with her, snug against her hip on the couch, like the Queen of England. "Here," she said to the girl.

She produced a small sketch of an eyeball framed by long, swooping eyelashes, and a single tear falling from the corner of the eye. "I see what's ancient in you," she said to the girl. "But you don't yet understand that life is harder for the searchers. You're still too light." She pressed the sketch into the girl's hand.

The Starlet

She cried softly on my shoulder.

"The depth of my sadness," she said as she wept more openly, "it's just... it's... I don't think you could understand. The depth of it." She wiped her nose with the back of her hand. I knew she would bring that snotty hand over to me, wipe her snot on my sleeve without thinking, leave her traces on me. I knew because I knew. The more likely someone is to make a mess, the less likely they are to clean it up. My life had taught me this.

The waiter gave me a conspiratorial look and a shrug. He gathered our empty plates and glasses. He nodded in the direction of my wine glass, asking if I intended to finish it. I put my hand over the glass. He understood I needed it. He blew out the candle at the center of the table and gave me one final look. *Your problem now.* I inhaled sharply. Prepared for what was coming.

Her tears were coming too fast now. She was losing her legendary composure. "I don't know if you know," between sobs.

"I don't know if I know either." I wished I had a cigarette. Tempted to roll my eyes, I drained the last of the red wine in my glass. She pushed her hair away from her face, lifted her head from my shoulder, repositioned her body. Face to face now. Here was the famous beauty. The face that brought millions to their knees.

I saw the fine bone structure that had launched a thousand Instagram filters. I saw the precise, careful work of the makeup artist who painted her face daily to confirm that her face was still the face the public needed it to be. I looked into those round, pleading eyes and decided I would stay. I'd make a night of it.

It wasn't my curiosity that made me stay. Not even my vanity. I could score so many points with so many of my worthless friends. But no, it was the absence in those pleading eyes. She was not safe. She was not well. The more I looked in those eyes, the more afraid I was for her. Who was looking after her? Who was checking in on her? How could they let her wander these streets unaccompanied?

She pulled out her phone. 247 unread text messages.

The Rabbi

"Did you hear? He died very suddenly." The women were gathered in a cluster, awaiting the start of the curriculum meeting.

Stifled disbelief, little muffled shrieks. Their cluster tightened, they pulled in on each other.

"It was a heart attack. No one could have seen it coming."

"But," one woman leaned in, lowered her voice a whisper, "you know what they found in his office? Pornography. *Lots*."

Lindsay Lerman

The Cursed Art of Storytelling

These sickly days, I desire so hard I give
myself migraines, pains that make me hallucinate

see visions, aches that fill my face like rain, but I
will not stop thinking about sex

during the past few years, I have only desired
three men, which makes me feel chaste

the only thing they have in common is that
they're all unavailable. This unholy trinity comprises

a gay man, a married man, and a bisexual twink.
The gay and the married are both thirty years older than me, but

I prefer them both to my decadent twink.
How this has happened is inexplicable to me.

I have to focus on the dead-end of my 9 to 9 job, but
I'm constantly vibrating, like my phone, a total whore

the married man sees me in public places
to talk about death and our favourite novels and

his wife calls 66 times during our two-hour novelistic talk.
He is apologetic, but I am so wet and thrilled I

don't mind. I rush to the public bathroom and
the evidence is clear – there is a flood.

When I return to our table, he asks
me if he makes me nervous as he strokes

my sweaty hands with his lithe fingers and dark eyes, and I suffice
to say *maybe*. I apologise for my sweat, slip

my hands away, and rant about my dead mother (again) and my strange

desires for the strange gay angel. Elsewhere, I tell my desired gay about

my desire for the confused twink and bore him to death.
At midnight, through the smokes of our wine,

I whisper to the twink that his scandalous story
is making me sick as I playfully

pretend to choke him; I profess his chaos excites and
sickens me as I pull his ponytail that falls apart in my palm.

He says we're just a typical pair of traumatised sluts in
need of morals as he gifts me a repressed kiss. Why do I do this?

This endless desire for unachievable pleasure,
for flirting so badly you make your crush vomit.

I need to throw away my life, reinvent myself through
masquerading my traumas as drama. I want to stop this existence and

Start all over again. A historic chance to change my name
my shame, my games, my pasts, presents, and the futures

Romanticism only works as a literary school, not a way of life.
When I was growing up, I should've read less literature

and other useless arts, instead I should've studied self-help
and survival tactics during capitalism and colonisation for people

with Byronic visions, Persian temperaments, wrong names,
wrong borders, wrong years, wrong sexes.

But I am also happy I don't have a penis, and sometimes I'm happy
I educated myself through Romanticism – not self-help –

there is no dichotomy, and I'm not looking down on anything, but
thank you very much I'd rather be a lost libertine than a 'thriving' liberal.

Still, I am an expert in denial. Wetness is my superior secret,
and I will take it to my grave before confessing my impure sensations.

Golnoosh Nour

Futures

Dancing leads to sex.

This is the official reason my High School will not be having a Prom. Instead, it will be a *Senior Banquet*. Respectable. *God honoring*. Without the distraction of dancing, we're thus saved from the doom of pre-marital sex.

Our school is tiny. Technically it's just a converted church/office space that took us in after our original campus got foreclosed by Wells Fargo in '98. No gym. No lab. No locker hall. No gays as far as I can tell. And now not even a fucking Prom.

Let me also explain that this is in San Francisco. Home of the studded belt, *not* the Bible belt; however, this only emboldens our teachers. One of them rails against the sinfulness of the city daily. He refers to gay men as "homophiles" and Tom Ammiano, an openly gay politician in the city, as "that flaming faggot". This is Bible class. The teacher, Mr. S, is tall and thin with a groomed gray mustache. He tucks his flannel into his medium wash blue jeans in exactly the way I've seen the spectral-like men who roam SoMa do it. Each and every one of them looks weathered—gnawed at--with eyes that point and poke upon whomever they contact. Only years later will I connect Mr. S's aesthetic to these ghostly men. Maybe, just *maybe*, Mr. S has had a "dance" or two back in his day.

Regardless, none of these mustached artifacts come close to the men I'm learning to desire.

Honcho. Torso. Blueboy. Playguy. Playgirl. Mandate. AllMan. Inches. Latin Inches. Black Inches.

Every corner store I enter my eye immediately goes to the magazine stand. I know which stores carry these treasures and which one's (pathetically) only have *Playboy*. The few magazines I've been able to "liberate" I must hide between my video game magazine collection at home—my only shred of privacy in the studio apartment I share with my mom. Alas, the corner stores are small. Cozy. The more I hover and loiter there, the more recognizable I become. I move my operation to bigger stores. Busier, more distractions. Ironically, these big-box bookstores don't even carry any juicy smut. My horny search takes me to a section simply called "Lifestyle". On the top row are titles like *Out* and *Genre* and *Instinct*—an interview with Melissa Etheridge, STI pop-quiz, best men's spas in Brazil. This is all great but where are the boners?

While decidedly less titillating, I still devour them. It's my first window into *gay culture*. This is years before my too cool "I'm not like other gays" 20's, when I'd consider those two words peak oxymoron. At this point it's still a new language to me. And I'm picking it up quickly. The first and most important dialect is *desirability*. White or white passing. Clean-cut. Sculpted features. The shirts, if present, are tight; the pants, if present, are *tighter*. Everything—sex, happiness, financial autonomy, the Brazilian men's spa— hover around the body. And this is only advertisements! The lesson is twofold: Not only am I to lust over a very specific man, but it's also painfully clear the only way to attain him is to *become* him. All the featured couples look exactly alike. Even the rare Black or Brown men somehow bend into the whiteness of their partner. At home in the mirror, I go over my 17-year-old self. It's like a frenzied checklist: no abs, no ass, non-colossal penis, and, to top it all off, BRACES.

A rough education. Yet it turns out to be the only education I get! Sex-Ed, in any official capacity, simply does not exist at my tiny private school. Liberal San Francisco can't touch Mr. S's agenda. We watch videos of "experts" proclaiming abstinence only, there's one about "evil temptresses" throughout history who led their noble men astray, and—most memorable— "cured" gay men now living wholesome lives with their exhausted looking wives. Condoms or "the pill" aren't mentioned anywhere. Abortion is practically a swear word. Cheesy as my "gay lifestyle" magazines are, they do form a sort of guide for me. Melissa Etheridge notwithstanding, every other page is an article on "safe sex". I glance around at all the wide-eyed straight students in my class. It occurs to me that these videos are all the education they'll get.

An article in *Instinct* gives a proper breakdown on cruising: make eye contact in passing, pause, look back after three seconds, if he also glances back then go for it honey! Walking the city at night isn't new to me. Increasingly it's my refuge from mom and the jail-cell sized apartment. Now I have a mission. I attempt eye contact with every man I pass, even if I don't find them particularly attractive. It's automatic. Often, they return the glance. Some for just an instant. But a few hold the stare: down and up, the once-over. Elevator eyes. That's when I flinch. Terrified. Head down, walking faster. So fast I find myself by the ferry building. A long-dotted horizon unspooling in hazy lights marks the Bay Bridge amidst the jet-black sky. The bay sloshes loudly. Invisibly. It's chilly. My mind swings from chaotic horny to frustration to just plain exhaustion. Exhausted by all these possible futures. Yet none of them add up. I keep thinking about those men on the video, these "ex-homophiles". Is that one future? *Cured.* The coldness crisps my thinking. No. I don't believe these men. Or want to be them. After all, how "ex-gay" can they be if they all still have their clone moustaches? That leaves me with…what? The Bay before me. Audible yet invisible—the only way to know it's truly there is to go under it. Submerge. Sink. Something is sketching into my mind. I don't recognize it yet. It's too new. For now it's just this moment, sitting here alone, staring at the black water. Staring at the potential for oblivion. Until it too becomes a future.

Zach Grear

Home is where you park your van (1994-2000)

Erik Moore

All the places I slept (more or less) in order of sleeping from June 2007–May 2008 while I was "travelling"

Seattle – my parent's guest room
Seattle – Mattie's place
SF – Julia's loft bed at 23rd and Valencia
SF – House sitting for Frances
SF – Meighan's studio while she was in Boston, the Mission
SF – The Holiday Inn at Fisherman's Wharf with Jordan
SF – Kevin and Jerry's place a.k.a The Vortex in the best possible Mission location
SF – The Westin Hotel
Ludlow, CA – some gas station hotel on my way to Tucson.
Flagstaff, AZ – Super 8 hotel still on my way to Tucson
Tucson – parent's condo
Tucson – Tom's bed
SF – couch in outer office.
Shared a room with Liz for Chris and Kara's wedding
SF – Chris and Kara's while they were on their honeymoon, Cole Valley
Tucson – my parent's condo
Los Angeles – Bel Air – Milo's friend Brent's place while Brent was in Australia. Brent once punched Anthony Michael Hall in the face – it made the Enquirer.
SF – The Vortex and...?
SF – Bernal Heights – an air mattress on Phil's floor
SF – a nest made of couch cushions on my office floor
SF – Chris and Kara's while they went skiing for a weekend
SF – twin bed, sublet from Jenny who works at Google in the Mission
SF – Renaissance Hotel with Tom. Disaster.
North Fork, CA – slice of foam on a twin bed at Dhamma Mahavana Vipassana Center
SF – Eric Orr room at Hotel des Arts
Kansas City, MO – Liz and Kent's guestroom (double blow up air mattress!)
Raleigh, NC – my dad's guest room
Wrightsville Beach, NC – my great aunt Kay and uncle Nelson's guest room

Toms River, New Jersey – my aunt and godmother Betsy and Uncle Peter's spare room
Green Point, Brooklyn – Sarah's guest couch
Williamsburg – Michael's air mattress
Manhattan – Jordan's bed
Queen Anne, Seattle – Deb's spare apartment in her condo
Richmond Beach, Seattle – Nancy's parent's bed
Shoreline, Seattle – on a sleeping pad on the floor of my parent's office. I had the flu.
Oakland – Buuck's garage/studio
Oakland – Caroline and Bryan's guest room while they were in Mexico.
Oakland – Ritchie Rich's place while he was in New York.
Oakland – New bed. My place. Home.

Bloodied but unbowed

*I'm too busy throwing glitter on myself to
step back from the mirror and give me the once over.*

- Jodie Harsh, promoter of 2 Too Much at Circus, London

Rose buds floating in a bowl. Time to move.
        Hot water? Or bored?

Sparkled, fierce, unglued.
          You would have shit, too.

Brittle handles, cracked spine, shedding.
          How many more times? This year?

These old feet – pretty toes and dry my soul.
          (Shut…shut…shut your fucking piehole.)

Sweet rust smell, those roses. And mold.
          Next time will be different next time he swore.

Rummy, hung, worn.
          Mourn more this defamiliarized room.

Is this shithole permanent?
        Yep. For now.

Katie Kurtz

Night Running

Not long into the pandemic, I started going for long runs at 3:30 or 4:00 in the morning. It wasn't a cure for my insomnia, but a way to escape the agitation I felt as I lay frozen in a state of fear about everything and nothing. I had tried remedial measures, such as going to bed before midnight and reducing screen time, but like everyone else, I was too entranced by the immolation of modern society (finally!) not to spend an hour or two scrolling through Twitter before drifting off. Or, in the attempt to return to sleep, I had explored deep breathing and meditation, counting backwards from 300 in intervals of three, vintage porn and masturbation, and ingesting various potions and supplements, but nothing worked. Each night, most often at 3:28 but not always, something startled me awake, leaving me awash in vague dread that lasted until sunrise, at which point I would slouch exhausted into the day.

But one summer morning, I was inspired for no reason I can remember to get up and look out the open window of my bedroom. I watched a cat saunter across the street. The regular din of stereos and car engines was absent. The street wasn't perfectly quiet, but what I heard was alluring. I listened to the quiet thud of a bass from a double-parked car with tinted windows, and it felt like a pulse. A siren arrived from another world. Could I find this world? As soon as I had asked the question, the answer appeared: why not.

There's something intoxicating about running down Riverside Drive—by which I mean the road itself and not the sidewalk—at four o'clock in the morning. There's no traffic. It's a dead time of night. If I hear an approaching vehicle, I have time to pull a little closer to the row of parked cars. But mostly there's nothing, which means my attention can wander. I'm always entranced by the traffic lights, which appear strangely beautiful as they flash uselessly from red to green in the summer mist that hovers above the empty street. Sometimes I see other people on the sidewalk, fading in and out of the streetlight like ghosts.

Before the pandemic, I preferred to run in the daylight. When I was a student, my track and cross-country teams always trained in the late afternoon. When I started an office job, I ran after work or sometimes at lunch. I sometimes heard co-workers talk about getting up at six in in the morning to run, but I—a career languisher—scoffed at the idea, which reeked of ambition and senior management. I also disliked the early sunsets of winter, when running in the dark meant dodging car traffic or tripping on cracks and potholes. I didn't want to worry about cars or wearing reflective clothing. I wanted the world to myself, which for me is the point of distance running.

Just north of Grant's Tomb, I veer back onto the sidewalk to a gap in the balustrade, revealing a large set of limestone steps. Pausing at the top, I observe the slow spiral that descends into the gloom like a stairway to hell. Even during the day, these steps, situated at the northern, disused, and decrepit end of a park, feel a little dangerous. If I am ever murdered on these steps, I'm sure that people will say, "well, what did he think would happen?" But being gay has taught me to disregard conventional wisdom about what—and where—is and isn't dangerous, particularly when such advice concerns the ruins of uptown Manhattan. Covered by brush and vines and mostly inaccessible to the police, these areas are havens for refugees of the day: the homeless, drug addicts, gay men cruising for sex, and—on this night—an insomniac on my way through the trees to the river.

At the Hudson, I turn north. The twin spires of the George Washington Bridge are draped in a string of white lights, but I am not only concerned with beauty at this hour: I am also thinking about death. I'm now fifty-four years old and I have no children who are not cats. Last year, my father was diagnosed with dementia and I—along with the rest of my family—have helped him to navigate the medical-industrial complex that dominates this final phase of his life. As daunting as it has been for him, I'm frequently left pondering the final phase of *my* life, which—even if I live into my eighties or nineties—is not so far away. How will I cope? Who will help when my body and mind start to go? Will it be the government? (Lol.) Should I start looking now for a young gay with whom I can make an "arrangement"? Or maybe I need to endear myself to a niece or nephew? Or should I consider another gay tradition, as a friend—also in his fifties, also with a father dying of dementia—recently suggested. What a relief it would be to go quickly. In the daytime, such thoughts would invite practical solutions, problem solving, and anxiety. But right now, I'm witnessing my own death as I run through this nocturnal landscape, and it is not so bad. It's not good, either. It just is.

I climb the hill to Fort Tryon, where I follow the narrow paths that traverse the darkest and cruisiest parts of the park. The men have all gone home by now—it's already close to five—but I know what's it like to walk in their shoes, and it's a good memory. The sky begins to lighten, suffusing the air with a silver glow that turns the heather into a tapestry of faint pink, red, and green. There are other flowers to admire at this time of year: the psychedelic purple allium, the clumps of echinacea that look like fireworks, and the cottony blooms of the oak-leaf hydrangea, each cluster of flowers jutting out from the bush like a thick, erect dick.

Matthew Gallaway

the rape raggedy tiara

home which
is a ham
burger
a dog lit
really
sees your
meal &
licks
their
lips

I had
a moment
of joy
on the
subway
after
I
went to the
eye doctor
I'm either
there
or not
in terms
of greatness
blow your
horn
he was good

and the
little bag
of grapes
wrapped
in paper
a nice
little pouch

I bought
on a
whim
I ate
them so
fast do
you do
that
there's something
about
the sweetness
of grapes
I almost
choke
dirty grapes
fast like
secret
sex
the best
nobody
knew about
that. My
own

the little pig
is dirty
on my
computer
it
was a
joke
I had
with you
or something
I got
from you
but you
didn't

get, the
holes
& the stones
she didn't
even notice
her daughter
was raped
what was
she dead
then not
now
the endlessly
alive
mother
the one in
charge
of anti
social
media
is losing
hers &
she's awful
to everyone
but
her crew
refuses
to mention
it. Being
loyal
to her loss.
But I
am loyal
to the loss
of the
present
the only
loss
worth
noting. I should
charge
you by the

minute
you pain
in the
ass. She's
going
she's
going
she's
gone. It's
winter &
I 'm
cooking vegetables
with
you that's
what I
miss &
giving you
holidays
like
a child.
The cowboy
rode
off
on Christmas

the rape
raggedy
tiara
everyone
goes. No
one
is a king.

Eileen Myles

Scarecrow

A scarecrow hangs from a plinth at a crossroads. He lives halfway between *other places* and the lives contained there, inside its buildings and streets. He could go this way or that but his twig-burst sleeves point both ways, the fabric flapping loudly in the crisp breeze. He paints a lonely figure to the travellers wandering past, glancing up at the blank expression crayoned onto a cloth sack: a crude facsimile given human form, a costume suspended in the night air. On the cover of Sonic Youth's album Bad Moon Rising, the silhouette of a scarecrow stands before the outline of a twilit city like some prophecy of a bad harvest, its pumpkin head burst into flames. He lives at the boundary of the metropolitan and pitch-black suburbia. He has nowhere to go but burn. Indecision is his song.

When I was ten-years-old, I played the Scarecrow in the school production of The Wizard of Oz. Tottering into the limelight, the Scarecrow draws on the dream of a face. He is naïve, unable to collect his thoughts. He speaks to the flowers. He wanders backwards and forwards like a *flâneur* in flannel. When Dorothy parts with her travelling buddies, she tells the Scarecrow, "I think I'll miss you most of all." I wonder if Dorothy grew to despise her Kansas farm and thought only of the Scarecrow living in exile, wandering dizzily across the poisonous wastelands of Oz. Maybe eventually, she loathed her relatives and saw their ways as small and mean-spirited. In dreams, she invoked a hurricane. The window of the house begins to rattle.

When I was older, I moved back into a family home for a short period. A scarecrow twists in the northern wind like a weathervane; his borrowed clothes, his windmill arms. I carried boxes of objects from apartment to apartment: birthday cards opened once; condoms never. The Shinto deification of the scarecrow is called Kuebiko, which translates as a "man who is falling apart." The god is paralysed but has complete awareness of its surroundings. A scarecrow becoming a statue. He stands, waiting in the tall grass. The villagers stitch his clothes with foul-smelling rubbish and tie loud cow bells onto his arms to frighten away the blackbirds. His ambition is ugliness.

In ancient Greece, wooden statues of Priapus watch over the crops beneath a blood red moon. Fertile protector of beehives, men pin their hopes to the well-endowed effigy. Autumn nights turning darker, the long months of hunger and poverty ahead. A Japanese village known as Nagoro has 35 inhabitants and more than 350 scarecrows. The locals peer from their windows at straw-filled counterparts. Tourists take photographs like autopsies of their pale skin. Mountain fog descends upon figures stood on the outskirts of each garden, across motionless bodies that can never belong, their naked arms stacked full of plum branches. They occupy a zone of the *intermediate*, dim souls without name or conclusion. A scarecrow leaves no grave.

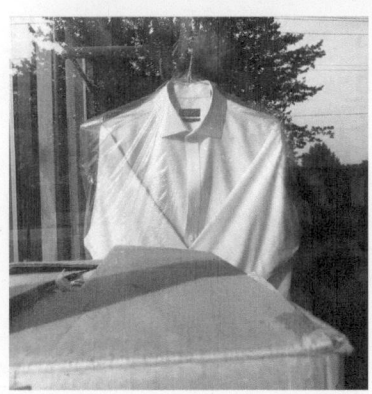

Matthew Kinlin and Neil Davies

Oh shirtless grandpa, where is your accident?
Collected Stickies 2013 – 2015

For two years, 2013-2015, I lived alone in a room in Rotterdam and lost my mind. My iBook had an application called "Stickies," and these are some of the notes that I wrote then.

I've seen the best minds of my generation lying around reading.

The Parable of the American Prosecutor: The American prosecutor went for a walk and he soon became thirsty. He stopped at a house to ask for a glass of water. The owner answered the door. The prosecutor said, "give me your house or I'll burn it to the ground." The owner went to court and said, "Judge, this man threatened to burn my house to the ground." And the American prosecutor said, "but I only wanted a glass of water."

The drunk loves potatoes.

You can't deny anything, ever. You can't even deny lies told about you. What's said is said and the rest, denying it, is repetition and further injury. To fight gives strength to whatever you're putatively opposing. I should be less polemical, stop writing *against*. Writing for can conjure new possibilities; it changes the subject.

I'm interested specifically in the absence of power—being with others without power. Notions of struggle or ideals or purity are unwelcome. They're all iterations of power. I want only the people present and our willingness to be together without power, our *indulgence*, I guess, of a Quixotic condition.

"Oublication" is, first, a typo, and second a neologism meaning any organized program of forgetting.

Roughly described, reading is the opposite of shopping. Shopping is pursuit, reading is surrender. Rather than shopping's pursuit, acquisition, and consumption, reading begins with surrender and proceeds without ambition, goals, usefulness or depletion toward sharing. We are changed by reading, but the text, what we read, is not. Shopping has a goal. Reading, none. Yet the two are not starkly separate. Window shopping is their love child.

"Down with the birds and the bees and the Viennese...brother let's stuff that dove, down with love..." Listening to Blossom Dearie's rendition of "Down With Love," I realize this is the first punk song, a brutal unrelenting attack on romantic illusions.

Oh shirtless grandpa, where is your accident? Halloween-Eve, New York City. God Damn. RIBLER-GMBH Business Contacts, Stuttgart, DE

The thing about being drunk and high all the time is that you get used to it, the same way that other people get used to being depressed or suicidal. You adjust. After a while it's obvious when you shouldn't be using a sharp knife or sending emails. Personal judgement is never impaired by a habit that's carried on long enough. Personal judgement returns no matter what curve balls you throw its way—so long as you are loyal for long enough to recalibrate. And no one is more loyal than an addict.

The thing about art is essentially the opposite. For example, you probably assume that for me to have written the first paragraph, I must be drunk and high all the time. But I'm not. Indeed, if I was, I could never have written it. Art is a reversing mirror, I think (though maybe I'm drunk or high) and it shows us what we live with everyday, turned strange. Strange enough to see, yet turned (or turning) enough that we are obliged to continually see it new, in some detail. Art is the curve ball that keeps on breaking.

Children are natural fascists, of course they are. They are, to their knowledge, recently borne of Gods and the world promises them everything. Only weakness will forestall their limitless triumph. As culture is infantilized and we all become infants, so we become fascists. This is the core engine of political change in the U.S. now.

No one wants to hear my gender theory, but here it is: Women created human society; men could give a shit. Left to themselves men would wander in packs, singing, fighting, and sucking endless cock. But women made human society, and then they domesticated the men. First they domesticated dogs. If the dogs could give them babies they wouldn't have bothered with the men. Men are a lot of bother. The hardest part is raising the boys. Naturally, boys become men, and this is an awkward, even terrifying, passage for the women. That perfectly malleable, sweet, hairless, adoring creature, the boy, turns some age and suddenly he is displaced, zombie-fashion, by a large, smelly, truculent, sperm-producing man who lies around the house and snaps at the women. The boy wants to be with the men, naturally, but instead the women must domesticate him—make him be "a man." It's not easy to do, so human society (which women created) denies the boy his autonomy for another five or six years (until he's eighteen) during which time he's a piece of property owned by the mother that can be made into a man. In fact there is no such thing as "a man." There is only "the men," that wandering, querulous, cock-sucking organism, and "a man" is a kind of animal-trick that women train the men to perform because the women need "a man" around the house to make babies. Human society's greatest struggle is this constant and unnatural dissolution of "the men," breaking them down into that horribly frustrated, destructive, and domesticated subject, "a man." Which is why men are such assholes who continually wreck society. Homo-sexuality is the only thing that keeps men from being total dicks.

The discouraging thing about death is the inevitable victory of the image. In death I will be superseded by an image; it is irresistible. The grinding inexorable victory of the image over life is enough to make me resist death. But that's foolish too. Better to try and infuse the image with life, while I can, so that what survives me is at least interesting.

HAIR-SPLITTING AT GOOGLE—"Promotions" vs. "Social."

Power is externalized fear. And anarchism is the repudiation of power. It is a specific politics that returns always to this refusal. I don't mean that power is those things that we do as a result of fear—attacks, subterfuge, revenge, etc.—I mean that fear is *a substance in our bodies*, an internal condition, and that it appears *as power* whenever we externalize it. Like water that becomes steam when heated in a vessel, fear, when it's driven from the body by our displeasure or intolerance of its presence in us, appears in the world as what we call "power." We exude power whenever we offload fear (usually through projection).

To witness a man's "power" or be caught by the "power" in a woman's gaze, is to see the raw fear exuded by their bodies, like steam rising from a runner's bare torso. They give off "power" as a consequence of having fear. It rises from them in catalyzing clouds at which we marvel. Uncritically externalizing fear, these people wield power. Anarchists repudiate this. An anarchist is not at ease either offloading fear or witnessing its transformation into power. Anarchism requires, first, that we become conscious of fear and able to manage its externalization.

A deep mindfulness about fear and its management is the prerequisite for anarchism. Fear can never be squelched nor erased—it can only become conscious and manageable. To repudiate power requires, above all, the conscious, critical management of fear and alternatives to its externalization. This is anarchism's starting place.

Literature is a superb tool for the conscious, critical management of fear, a way to mitigate its externalization. It is, in fact, probably our best cultural tool for this. Science and religious faith (to name two of our strongest cultural tools) coddle fear and abet its uncritical externalization. Literature does not. The anarchist must learn to read, and be a supple, nimble reader. It won't help for the anarchist to memorize dogma or prove theses, etc., etc. It will help her more to read novels and to laugh and cry.

Europe: a continent of nomads trapped in architecture. They'd much rather be in caravans moving freely from campground to campground, from sea coast to lake-shore to mountains. But civilization "saved" them from the Huns, the Roma, the gypsies. Give them freedom and they'll spend it camping. The European hatred of the Roma is a toxic stew of projection and envy, a key to the European condition.

Matthew Stadler

Double

Fisher Main

Reliable

Come, let's peer over the precipice:
how I cancelled out
the space you were in. Flying the flags
that sent our pain away for those moments
like tourists when we both dropped in.
Possibly, if you looked within
you would find three bobbins
and an old sewing machine. An outdated
infrastructure to repair my
own skin. Hear the medal pedal
whirring worrying
the situation I find myself in.
What did my laughter
sound like to you-
a trilling of tongue, dissected
with a too low dose of medicine?
The use of a robot
in the heart of a forest
guessing the name of the
fruit of temptation?
Parts can't be found
or taken for granted-
always useful when a breakdown's
expected-

Ranee Zaporski

statuette

children hung keys in the garden   a toy car
    a garland of the heads of petunias
which begged for death   being neuter & out of place
    anyhow   i gave up my charm   the head of a fish
made of mother of pearl   a frosted-glass lamp
    the last years of my youth to celibacy

dog dug a hole   hole stayed
    block of cheese on the counter
      slice of ham   few eggs
    the boy's face quick with solitude
i watched him   my lips the lips of a medusa
    turned backwards   the mirror
the slump of serpents to earth
    no longer hungry   sluggish

            hungry
i pressed my lips to the line about
    a strong man pressing his tongue into a granite head
cat fought the neighbor's cock in the night
    and the scent of petunias   don't belong here
a stranger pointed out a change in my face
    i sat very still   i sat in the light
drank pomegranate juice instead of liquor
    there was a blue curve of

a blue house in the outfield
    and the walls came to a point
and the nails all fell out
    and he never loved me anyhow
and i lived in a lot of attics
      a blue one   another blue one
        a pink one   and i loved them

    i already set the table

jimmy cooper

Salaried

I tried to do this whole thing again. After I was laid off during the pandemic, I told myself that I would never work for a place again that tries to wrap your individual identity with its corporate self. It seems like that sort of thing sneaks up on people like a snake. And once someone is bitten, it's as if they enjoy the venom. They don't even realize that they are now paralyzed.

When I got a new job in management at a trendy dine-in movie theater, I thought, this could be my balance: combining the professional with an interest, as I do classify myself as a cinephile. At first everything was fine, although my hours were wonky and I started taking light sleeping pills. That was months ago. Since then, I was put on salary, which they acted like I should bend down and thank them for. When I was no longer an hourly, the General Manager (a man whose sexuality I cannot determine, although he does present as closeted), who also has restaurant jargon tattooed on his arm, told me that when someone "goes on salary, you basically become a servant."

Then, my hours changed…drastically. I was working close to 60 hours a week, twelve hours a day and was expected, really, to be on call. My schedule could change at any time. I started feeling less like myself and rightfully so. I wasn't creating as much art as I once was. My husband, who, trust me, has always heard me lament (it's who I am), now saw me drained in a way that made me look and feel hollow, you might say. Then, my coping skills, they too began fading away.

Every day, every single day, servers at work would come up to me and tell how overworked they were. They told me that their bodies hurt and that mentally, they were just getting by. They were working up to 12-hour shifts in sold out theaters, going up and down stairs to deliver heavy trays of food and drink. I couldn't help them; I couldn't supply the bodies that would be needed to support that amount of labor. I tried to help, and I tried to advocate for myself, too.

When I pulled the General Manager aside, I said, "What I need, and I think what everyone needs, is some sort of balance between work and life. I need to feel healthy."

I mentioned this to him because that day he expected me to close the building for the night, getting out past 2 am, to wake up and then attend a boozy-ass staff party at 11 am, which was nearly an hour away from where I live and then to return to work and close out the night again.

When I told him I cannot do all of that, he snickered and said, "Why, do you need your beauty sleep?"

Later, I had what they call an after shift drink (which always sounded so corny to me) at the bar once my work day or night was over. It's hard to leave when you're there for so long and your mind is clouded and then there's alcohol waiting. From there, I went with a coworker to another bar down the street, most likely having shots of whiskey and beer. Then I walked to a hole-in-the-wall kind of bar, which was on the way home, where I met a woman who I guess used to be in the New York club scene in the early 2000s. We bonded over bumps of coke in the bathroom. By the time we left, it was almost 6 am.

The only thing is, I wasn't going home, not yet. I walked to a sex / video/ DVD sex booth store or whatever you want to call it. There was an open room with black walls and couches and gay porn playing on an old TV overhead. I had been there before but I never stayed for long. I've always been curious about, I'm not sure, what you don't see, what lies beneath, what is I guess considered underground. Tonight, there was a beautiful young man, who looked Brazilian, who was built and caramel, and was butt-naked jerking off. Surrounding him were four Black men, older, heavier, with their cocks out. He started sucking on all of them, taking turns on each, feverishly twisting his mouth around them. I wanted to join, to be a part of whatever this hedonistic voyage was. I stripped off all my clothes and watched. In the corner, I spotted someone jerking off, a white punk-ish dude with colorful Doc Martens. He motioned for me to sit on the edge of his leg, which I did. I sat there, balancing on his knee. Then I stood up, and he squirted lube on his cock and I slid gently down letting him enter me.

I'm assuming a few minutes later (my sense of time was not the strongest at this point), I dressed and took a cigarette break outside when the Doc wearing man made his exit. He and I did not even look at one another. He crossed the street, running against traffic, going along his way. Me though, I wasn't done, not yet. I went back inside and I joined the Brazilian dude, and the four or five men around him and the both of us took as many cocks as we could. Our throats open, our chins upward, we let all of them fuck our throats. I found someone then that I wanted, for myself. He was about 50 years old, had a biker build with Black smooth skin and a white beard. He took me to a stall or booth and I told him, "I want to cum while sucking your dick." He smiled, put a glass pipe to my mouth, and I inhaled and took him as deep in my throat as I could.

And now I ask: Is there a way, any way, in this capitalistic country that loves to punish, is there any way not to explode?

Jason Haaf

s.w.? (-a.w.)

milk skin, creased as an eyelid
drifts on the surface of coffee.

a summer in berlin, cadmium
and copper speak.

a chicken bleeds so
dogs can eat. seeds clutch

at grassy knobs. cardboard welts
the soil. a prairie browns, and roots
furl in.

a man thinks
it's made for him. iron teeth
make rank through mud.

so what if i hid from you,
so what if i cried beneath blankets,
so what if i cycled through your same mistakes,
over and over, the fabric continues to flame.
so what if i was in love?

did it hurt you?

your trauma met
hers on the street and
hung its shackles.

hope a yearning breech.
yet plaster and piñon
burn to curtain.

fingers clasp another's, as thousand-armed
gods have done before,

believe their suffering to be
special, to deny as their first god died,
yearning, as all animals do

there is a window in the roof,
square and small, blinking bright after a storm.
how the blue can cut you open. so
open it.

marriage

Bone white in deep blue. Drone sounds sew
through. She struggles now to cope,

nerves betray their maker. I want
to walk, farther and farther away,

every day. Everything about you
laced with a threat. On weekends,

sweet lemon loaf lodged between
the soft crotch of tiny knuckles,

heard the diving bell, recoiled
at the mealy sounds of mother's mouth.

Masc turnt belly up, hair growing
coarser year by year. We plunge, deeper

into the system. Its opacity beckons
us like a gleam. Impossible depths.

Maybe it never ends. Maybe we see a light.

Radiation bleeds through the stratum
like a bruise. Its sybilline heat.

Bubbles rise and we just keep
breathing. So what.

Elle Nash

Leisure Class

1.

I'm in an abusive relationship with time. It's been a week since I left my apartment. I'm embarrassed to say it but not to live it.

I wouldn't call my self-exile from society a withdrawal. I've been through withdrawal a few times and that was about missing something, wanting something I couldn't have anymore. I do not feel that way about people.

2.

When I was young, I moved so frequently every address was a forwarding address. My broken heart then was my family. Now it's everything else: the faint echo of all the other ones. A friend calls this The Chamber. A room one enters where the present and the past are if not indistinguishable, than blurred beyond recognition.

You're peripatetic someone once said. I knew of people who called themselves travelers and were always looking for adventure. They were living life to the fullest. What I mean is they had money. Not on them. Back home. Money from home. I didn't have money and the people back home didn't have money and they didn't want to hear from me anyway. I was a wanderer, a shirker, an in-betweener. I was a fagabond.

3.

Home has been such a strange word for me. I have referred for years to where I grew up as a child as my mother's home. It's a distinction that flies past most people but sticks out to the right ones.

Fifteen. The summer before I left the house I grew up in, my mother drove in silence and I talked. We were going in circles. That building was definitely on repeat. We were lost but she wouldn't admit it. I stopped talking so she could focus, as if she had been paying attention to me, as if that was the problem. Finally, she said, "This isn't working." I thought she meant the drive. Then it hung in the dusted air: Us. Me and her. My mother was working up to dumping me.

After I left, my mother told people I'd ran away. She didn't want to be the woman who kicked her queer kid out, so she got to be abandoned. I didn't want to be a victim, the kid thrown out of his mom's house. What good would that do me? At best, a bed somewhere for a little while with a blanket of pity. At worst, the kind of vampires who smell desperation and descend. We both got what we wanted.

4.

As someone who spent years having to code switch and lie to survive, when I hear people brag about their authenticity and honesty I hear *privileged and lazy*.

5.

All the years of ricocheting around have left a permanent mark. I will always be restless. When I was younger, I thought it was bad, a character flaw of some kind. But I've witnessed the way people cave in, lard up, and dull down. I know I'm not ready for that slow death march. I still want things, ridiculously small yet unlikely dreams I've kept flickering for twenty years. I can maybe have something turn out. Something so tiny it won't change anything. Why not? People have crazier and more mundane plans they turn into crusades trumpeting through lives.

6.

Another move, another unpack: I look through a box and find the book of poems I wrote when I was fifteen during three weeks in the psych ward. The only writers' retreat I've ever attended. That book was a promissory note. I find an envelope of photos and slides of me at sixteen with a bleached blonde grown-out mohawk. I suppose this is the moment where someone my age says, "Who was that person?" or smiles with amusement at their youth, but I feel all that rage and fear still, fresh as ever. A fact more real than this box. I have seen people post pictures of themselves laughingly from their pasts. I *thought I was so punk*, says the caption, written from an office or home somewhere safer, distant. I scroll through their vacation and food photos and think, How boring. And then: How did I waste my time on people kill-ing theirs until their marriages, mortgages, and affairs arrived.

7.

M tells me I'm not working-class. To him, working-class means a CNC machinist.

I look at my reflection in the Coinstar screen and say, "Elite."

8.

How do I talk to a person who has never been so hungry they've considered mugging someone? Whoever said there is no such thing as bad publicity had family money.

9.

Val had a rich boyfriend and a monthly allowance he referred to as "walking around money." I believe it was four thousand. That's a hell of walk. Of course, the boyfriend and the allowance came to an end. There was some sort of severance payment, and then Val drifted around New York for a year or two, making and breaking plans, reeling in and throwing back suitors of means. Eventually he left for a trip to California and didn't return. Rumors of Los Angeles and hard, harder, and hardest drugs followed, as well as tidbits about ashrams and a desert community of artists. Then a few years ago walking uptown I thought I saw Val, a version of him with a tautened face, eating in a bistro. The face looked at me, the space of maybe a glance, and looked away quickly. Recognition or not. Val or not. I wasn't sure and I quickened my pace.

10.

My subconscious is not subtle: Dreams of lottery winnings, expensive boots, and rough sex. Where are those cryptic encoded ones other people share? Or are they lying?

11.

They swim smugly with the current in a river dug for them and tell us how easy it is. They wear $500 Heritage work boots in black cherry leather and $300 plaid shirts. Class anxiety is expensive.

12.

Catered for young rich people today. Home now, changed into my nightshirt, lantern turned low, telling the shadows about how Marie Antoinette stepped on her executioner's foot walking to the guillotine. Her last words: "Pardonnez-moi, monsieur." The shadows love that story.

13.

Dear Citibank: I assure you the Credit Score you are offering may be free but it will not be complimentary.

14.

I am an institutionally illegitimate person and I conduct myself accordingly. When I think of who are considered credible witnesses and reliable sources and *good* people, I don't want to be aligned with them. I'll stay over here with the ex-cons and former junkies and dropouts and fuckups.

15.

There aren't enough hours in the day to say no to all the all the things I don't want to do.

16.

I worked brunch and am now icing my knees and praying to Satan for sleep or sudden death. The shift was both boring and fraught. A young coworker referred to me as a seasoned pro in a way that suggested a past rife with drifters who tipped in venison and scratch-off lottery tickets. I overheard a man say, "If there is a No Firearms sign, I get back in my truck and go somewhere else. The missus and I don't eat in free fire zones." The cokehead line cook said dairy congested him. He explained how wheat turned to sugar in the body and how sugar broke down collagen and accelerated aging. He looked right at me. I excused myself to smoke.

17.

The name of the envoy Queen Victoria dispatched to meet Karl Marx: Sir Mountstewart Elphinstone Grant Duff.

18.

I want to run away and leave everything. I check my bank account and settle for cold pizza and a book.

19.

The oldest story: an insider pretends to be an outsider and receives praise for his empathy and imagination and intelligence. Maybe some asshole even says bravery. An outsider pretends to be an insider, is exposed as a fraud, a liar, and burned to the ground.

20.

Time and again I outwitted my destiny. I freed myself from my family of farmers and factory workers. My faggotry was my passport. It allowed me to rise above my social class. I dodged the boredom of its implicit victimhood through rage and drugs. I moved constantly. I evaded community and friends who wanted to replicate family roles. I left jobs and towns. I didn't stay in touch. And I told myself this manifesto every time life was particularly brutal and pointless: I made myself, unmade myself, started over from scratch. I am my own creator, so yes I do believe in god.

21.

That's the deck. This is the hand. What can you do?

Nate Lippens

Contributors

jimmy cooper
Neil Davies
Matthew Gallaway
Zach Grear
Jason Haaf
Matthew Kinlin
Katie Kurtz
Lindsay Lerman
Nate Lippens
Fisher Main
Erik Moore
Eileen Myles
Elle Nash
Golnoosh Nour
Matthew Stadler
Ranee Zaporski